Fun Fan Facts:
The Unofficial NBA Edition

Philadelphia 76ers

Everything Young 76ers Fans Should Know

By: Jake Liam

Dedication

For every Philly kid who ever screamed "Trust the Process" and somehow actually meant it.

And for everyone in Philadelphia who has been waiting for a championship since 1983. You've been patient. Sort of.

THE NBA BY THE NUMBERS

MOST NBA CHAMPIONSHIPS[*]

- CELTICS (18) [†]
- LAKERS (17)
- WARRIORS (7)
- BULLS (6)
- SPURS (5)

As of the 2024-25 Season. †One Trophy = 4 Championships.

NBA HISTORY SNAPSHOT

1946	1954	1979	2023
NBA Founded	Shot Clock Introduced	3-Point Line Added	NBA Cup Introduced

BIG NUMBERS

$156 million
Stephen Curry's est. earnings in the 24-25 season

7'7"
Tallest player in NBA history (Gheorghe Mureșan & Manute Bol)

30 | 4 | 82

30 Teams Competing in the NBA

4 Playoff Rounds

82 Games Per Season

PHILADELPHIA 76ERS IN THE NBA

- FOUNDED: 1946[†]
- NBA TITLES: 3
- CONFERENCE TITLES: 5[*]

52 Playoff Appearances

*† Founding dates are complicated & may cause arguments at Thanksgiving. Ask someone born before color TV. All Titles reflect pre-relocation franchise history. * As of 2024-25 Season.*

NBA ALL-TIME MVP LEADERS

KAREEM ABDUL-JABBAR (6) ★ MICHAEL JORDAN (5) ★ BILL RUSSELL (5)

EASTERN CONFERENCE

- Atlantic – **Celtics**
- Atlantic – **Nets**
- Atlantic – **Knicks**
- Atlantic – **76ers**
- Atlantic – **Raptors**
- Central – **Bulls**
- Central – **Cavaliers**
- Central – **Pistons**
- Central – **Pacers**
- Central – **Bucks**
- Southeast – **Hawks**
- Southeast – **Hornets**
- Southeast – **Heat**
- Southeast – **Magic**
- Southeast – **Wizards**

WESTERN CONFERENCE

- Pacific – **Lakers**
- Pacific – **Clippers**
- Pacific – **Warriors**
- Pacific – **Suns**
- Pacific – **Kings**
- Northwest – **Nuggets**
- Northwest – **Timberwolves**
- Northwest – **Thunder**
- Northwest – **Trail Blazers**
- Northwest – **Jazz**
- Southwest – **Mavericks**
- Southwest – **Rockets**
- Southwest – **Spurs**
- Southwest – **Pelicans**
- Southwest – **Grizzlies**

Introduction

Welcome, fans! Whether you're new to cheering for the Philadelphia 76ers or you've been bleeding the team colors your whole life, this book is packed with fun, exciting facts about your favorite team. Get ready to impress your friends and family with everything you know about the 76ers.

Quick Time Out

This book is packed with stats. Like, A LOT of stats. Every fact was checked, double-checked, and triple-checked. But here's the thing about basketball history: not everyone agrees on everything. Ask someone who watched games before color TV and someone who grew up with instant replay and you'll get two completely different answers. My dad, stepdad, uncle, and grandpa all argued about the same fact. Four people. Four answers. All of them think they're right. So if you spot something that doesn't match what you've heard, congratulations. You might be a bigger fan than the people who helped make this book. And honestly? That's pretty cool.

HOW IT WORKS

THE SEASON
82 Games. One Goal.
Each team plays 82 games.
Win enough to make the
Playoffs.
Every game counts!

PLAYOFFS
30 Teams. 16 Make It.
8 per conference make the playoffs.
Win=Advance | Lose=Go Home
Best record
gets home court!

PLAYOFF ROUNDS
Best of 7. Win 4 or Go Home.
4 rounds of pure pressure.
Every series is do-or-die!

OVERTIME?
5 More Minutes.
Keep playing until
someone pulls ahead.
No ties. Ever.

THE FINALS
One Series. One Champion.
Winner lifts the Trophy.
Legend status unlocked.

How the NBA Works

At first glance, basketball feels simple. Ten players. One ball. Two hoops. Go.

Then the NBA adds the layers.

An 82-game regular season. A draft where bad teams pick first. Playoffs that last two full months. Superstars who can change everything with one trade. Dynasties that rise, fall, and rise again.

And somehow, it all works.

The NBA is built on one big idea: every team gets a chance to reset, reload, and rise again. No relegation. No dropping down to a lower league. Just basketball, every night, from October through June.

It is a league designed for drama, stars, and comebacks. And once you understand the flow, it is impossible to stop watching.

The League Setup

The NBA has 30 teams, spread across the United States and Canada. Those teams are split into two conferences:

- Eastern Conference
- Western Conference

Each conference has three divisions, mostly based on geography. Divisions matter for scheduling, but not as much as they used to.

Every team plays 82 regular season games, usually from October through April. Home games. Road games. Back-to-back nights. Long road trips. The season is a marathon before the sprint even starts.

Win games, and you climb the standings. Lose too many, and the pressure builds fast.

How Games Are Played

An NBA game has four quarters, each lasting 12 minutes. That means 48 minutes of game time, plus timeouts, free throws, and the occasional coach argument that adds another 20 minutes nobody planned for.

Scoring is simple:

- A shot inside the three-point line is worth 2 points
- A shot beyond the arc is worth 3 points
- Free throws are worth 1 point

If the score is tied at the end of regulation, the game goes to overtime, which lasts 5 minutes. Still tied? Another overtime. Keep going until someone wins.

There is a shot clock too. Teams have 24 seconds to take a shot. No standing around. No holding the ball forever. Keep it moving.

The Regular Season Race

The regular season is long for a reason. It tests everything.

Depth. Health. Focus. Patience.

Teams play opponents from both conferences, but they face conference rivals more often. By the end of the season, each conference's top teams have earned their playoff spots the hard way.

The goal is simple: make the playoffs. But there is a twist.

The NBA Cup

In 2023, the NBA added something new to the middle of the season. Something with actual stakes. They called it the In-Season Tournament, now known as the NBA Cup.

It works like this: Every team plays a small group stage during November and December, with special court designs that look like nothing else in basketball. The best teams advance to a knockout round held in Las Vegas.

The winners split a prize pool. Players earn bonus money. And for the first time, a team could lift a trophy before the playoffs even started.

Some fans are still warming up to it. Some players love it. But the moment a team starts treating it seriously and a crowd shows up buzzing in December, it feels like something.

Which, honestly, sounds about right.

The Play-In Tournament

Instead of sending the top eight teams from each conference straight to the playoffs, the NBA added something new. The Play-In Tournament.

Here is how it works:

- Teams ranked 1 through 6 in each conference are safe
- Teams ranked 7 through 10 fight for the final two playoff spots

The 7 and 8 seeds have an advantage. Win once and you are in. Lose and you still get one more shot. The 9 and 10 seeds have to win twice in a row just to earn a first-round matchup.

It turns the end of the season into a sprint. Every game suddenly matters more. Fans love it. Coaches age rapidly.

The NBA Playoffs

Once the playoffs begin, everything tightens.

Sixteen teams enter. Eight from each conference. Every round is a best-of-seven games series. That means the first team to win four games moves on:

- First Round
- Conference Semifinals
- Conference Finals
- NBA Finals

Home-court advantage matters. Crowds get louder. Rotations get shorter. Superstars play heavier minutes. One bad quarter can flip a series. One great performance can define a career.

By the time the NBA Finals arrive in June, only two teams are left. One from the East. One from the West. Four wins away from a championship. Four wins away from history.

The NBA Draft: Hope Begins Here

Here is where the NBA gets clever. Every summer, new players enter the league through the NBA Draft. Teams take turns selecting college players, international stars, and teenagers straight out of high school.

The teams that finished with the worst records get the best odds to pick early through the Draft Lottery. It is not guaranteed, but it gives struggling franchises a real shot at changing their future with one pick.

That means one bad season does not doom you forever. It might actually change everything. Some franchises are rebuilt by a single draft night moment.

Hope shows up wearing a new jersey.

No Relegation. All Pressure.

Unlike many global sports leagues, NBA teams never drop down to a lower league. They always stay in the NBA.

That does not mean there is no pressure.

Fans remember losing seasons. Owners make changes. Coaches get replaced. Players get traded. Every year is a test of direction, patience, and belief.

Stars, Systems, and Showtime

The NBA is famous for its stars. But stars do not win alone.

Teams need chemistry. Coaches need systems. Role players need to deliver on the biggest stages. One injury. One hot streak. One trade deadline deal. Any of it can flip a season.

That balance between individual brilliance and team basketball is what makes the league special.

Fast breaks. Buzzer-beaters. Game 7s. And moments that get replayed forever. That is the NBA.

Once you get the flow, it is pure electricity.

Philadelphia 76ers Facts

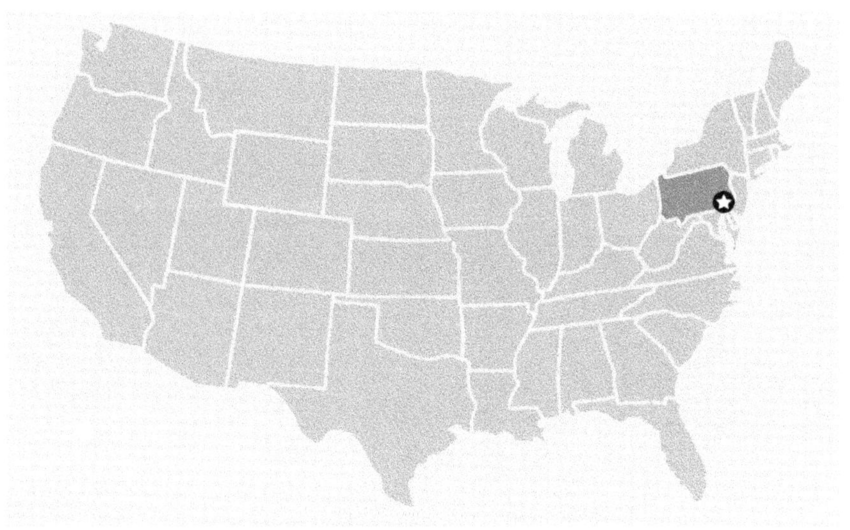

Home City

Philadelphia, Pennsylvania

Metro Area Population

About 6.2 Million

Home Arena

Wells Fargo Center

Arena Capacity

20,478

Conference / Division

Eastern Conference / Atlantic Division

Famous Local Food

Philly Cheesesteak, Soft Pretzels, Water Ice, Hoagies

Chapter 1: From Syracuse to the City of Brotherly Love

1. Born in Syracuse: The Nationals (1946)

Here is a fun thing to say at your next 76ers watch party: the team you are rooting for was not born in Philadelphia. It was not even born in a city most people can find on a map without squinting. The franchise that would become the 76ers started life in 1946 in Syracuse, New York, a place better known for snowstorms than superstars.

The Syracuse Nationals joined a scrappy new league that would eventually become the NBA, and they played in a building that held a few thousand people who showed up loud and stayed loud. No giant scoreboards. No light shows. No playlist blasting between plays. Just basketball, wooden floors, and fans who acted like every regular season game was Game 7 of the Finals. Because in Syracuse, it kind of felt that way.

Back then, players made so little money that most of them worked regular jobs in the offseason. A guy might drop 30 points on a Tuesday night and spend Wednesday selling insurance. The NBA was new, uncertain, and nobody knew if it would survive. The Nationals not only survived. They built a foundation tough enough to eventually carry an entire city on its back.

2. Champions First: The 1955 NBA Title

The 76ers have three championship banners. Most fans know about 1967 and 1983. The one that gets forgotten is the one that came first, before there were even any 76ers. The Syracuse Nationals won the 1955 NBA title, beating the Fort Wayne Pistons four games to three in a series that went all the way to a deciding Game 7. On their home floor. In front of a crowd that had been waiting their entire basketball lives for that moment.

The man who made it happen was Dolph Schayes, a forward who could shoot from the outside at a time when most big men acted like the three-point line was a personal insult. Schayes was relentless. He played through injuries that would have sent other players straight to the bench. In the 1952 playoffs he played with a broken wrist and still performed. The guy was basically allergic to sitting down.

Imagine this: it is 1955, television is barely a thing, and a team from upstate New York just won the world championship of basketball. No confetti cannons. No elaborate trophy presentation. Just a group of guys who outworked everybody else for an entire season finally getting to call themselves the best. That trophy belongs to this franchise. Every single 76ers fan owns a piece of it.

3. A New City, a New Name, and a Big Idea (1963)

By the early 1960s, the Nationals had a problem that no amount of winning could fix. Syracuse was small. The NBA was growing fast, chasing bigger cities, bigger arenas, and bigger paychecks. The owners looked at the math and made the call: Philadelphia or bust.

Moving to Philadelphia made basketball sense immediately. The city was enormous, passionate, and already bleeding sports. Eagles fans were intense. Phillies fans were intense. Philly fans are intense about everything, including the weather. Basketball fit right in.

But the name had to go. So the new owners did something genuinely cool. They opened it up to the fans, held a naming contest, and let the city decide. The winner was the 76ers, a direct reference to 1776, the year the Declaration of Independence was signed right there in Philadelphia. Think about that for a second. Every other team in American sports is named after an animal, a job, or a weather event. The 76ers are named after the birth of the entire country. In the actual city where it happened. That is not a team name. That is a flex.

4. Wilt Chamberlain Comes Home (1965)

Wilt Chamberlain had already done things on a basketball court that seemed physically impossible before he ever wore a 76ers uniform. He had grown up in Philadelphia, become a sensation at the University of Kansas, and entered the NBA with the Philadelphia Warriors. Then the Warriors packed up and moved to San Francisco in 1962, taking Wilt with them. The city of Philadelphia watched their best basketball player disappear to the other side of the country and had absolutely nothing to say about it.

Three years later, the 76ers made it right. In January 1965 they traded for Wilt and brought him home. He was 7 feet 1 inch tall, weighed 275 pounds, and ran the floor like a guard. Opposing centers would look up at him during warmups and have what can only be described as a very bad morning. Nobody in the history of the sport had ever combined that size with that speed, and Philadelphia had him back.

His 100-point game had happened in 1962 as a Warrior, and we will get to that story shortly because it absolutely deserves its own spotlight. What Wilt brought to the 76ers was something beyond statistics. He brought the feeling that the Boston Celtics, who had won eight straight NBA titles, were no longer unbeatable. Philadelphia had a weapon now. And Boston knew it.

5. The Greatest Team Nobody Talks About: 1966-67 (68-13)

Say the words "greatest team in NBA history" and most people immediately say the 1995-96 Chicago Bulls, who went 72-10 with Michael Jordan looking like a human highlight reel for an entire season. That is a completely reasonable answer. It is also an answer that completely ignores the 1966-67 Philadelphia 76ers, who went 68-13 and ended the longest dynasty in league history without breaking much of a sweat.

This team was absurd. Wilt Chamberlain at center, Hal Greer running the offense like a machine that never malfunctioned, Billy Cunningham coming off the bench and playing like he had a personal grudge against every player on the other team, and Chet Walker hitting shots from spots on the floor that made defenders question their entire career choices. It was not a superstar carrying four passengers. It was five guys who genuinely trusted each other and made every opponent feel completely overmatched.

They swept through the playoffs, knocked out the Boston Celtics and their eight straight championships, and closed out the NBA Finals in six games. The 1967 title is the one that still echoes. It is the banner that every great 76ers team since has been measured against. Seventy years of basketball later, that record regular season still stands as one of the greatest single-season performances in the history of the sport. Philadelphia built something that year that nobody has fully matched since.

Chapter 2: The Legends Who Wore Red, White, and Blue

6. Wilt Chamberlain: The Big Dipper (1965-1968)

There is a version of this chapter where we spend every single fact talking about Wilt Chamberlain and still not cover everything. He was that ridiculous. Wilt stood 7 feet 1 inch tall, weighed around 275 pounds, and had a wingspan so wide that he could basically guard two positions at once just by standing still and holding his arms out. Opposing coaches would draw up their game plans, look at Wilt's statistics, and then stare at the ceiling for a long time.

The 100-point game happened on March 2, 1962, in Hershey, Pennsylvania, while Wilt was still a Philadelphia Warrior. He scored 100 points in a single NBA game. Not 60. Not 70. One hundred. The next closest single-game record is 83 points, set by Miami Heat center Bam Adebayo in March 2026. Wilt beat that by 17 points. He made 36 of 63 field goal attempts and 28 of 32 free throws, which means he was also getting fouled constantly and still scoring 100 points anyway.

As a 76er he averaged 24 points and 24 rebounds per game in the 1966-67 championship season and made the entire team better by commanding so much defensive attention that everyone else got easier looks. He did not just play basketball. He warped the game around himself. Every rule the NBA changed during his era, they changed because of him.

The Night Wilt Broke the Scoreboard. In 1962, Wilt Chamberlain scored 100 points in one game. Fans didn't even have a proper sign to celebrate it, so someone grabbed a piece of paper and wrote "100." That homemade sign turned into one of the most legendary photos in sports. *Photo: Wilt Chamberlain after his 100-point game (1962). Public domain. Source: Wikimedia Commons.*

7. Julius Erving: Dr. J (1976-1987)

Before Julius Erving arrived in Philadelphia, most NBA basketball happened below the rim. You dribbled, you passed, you shot, you set screens. The game was beautiful but it was mostly horizontal. Dr. J changed the address. He took the game vertical and made things happen in the air that nobody had thought to try yet.

The ABA was a rival basketball league, and in 1976 it folded. Several of its teams got absorbed into the NBA, and the 76ers moved fast. They paid three million dollars to bring Erving over from the New York Nets, which was a jaw-dropping number at the time. He was 6 feet 6 with hands so big he could palm a basketball like most people palm a tennis ball. When he got going toward the basket, something happened that the NBA had never quite seen before. He would leave the ground earlier than anyone expected, stay up longer than physics suggested was fair, and finish at the rim in ways that made the crowd forget they were supposed to be watching a sport and not a magic show.

He played eleven seasons in Philadelphia, made the All-Star team every single year, and won the NBA MVP award in 1981. He also made a play in the 1980 NBA Finals against the Los Angeles Lakers that we will talk about in Chapter 3, because it is one of those moments that deserves a spotlight and a moment of silence. Dr. J did not just play for the 76ers. He gave the city something to believe in during a decade when championships were hard to come by.

8. Moses Malone: The Chairman of the Boards (1982-1986)

The 76ers had Julius Erving. They had Maurice Cheeks. They had Andrew Toney, who opposing point guards genuinely dreaded defending. They had talent everywhere. What they did not have was someone who could absolutely bully their way to the basket, grab every rebound in sight, and make the other team feel physically exhausted just from watching him work. Then they got Moses Malone, and the missing piece was no longer missing.

Moses Malone came to Philadelphia in the summer of 1982 as a free agent, signing what was at the time one of the richest contracts in NBA history. He had already won an MVP award in Houston. He was one of the greatest offensive rebounders the league had ever produced, which meant that when a shot went up and missed, Moses was already in position to put it back in before the defense had finished processing what happened. He averaged more than 15 rebounds per game in his first Philadelphia season. Fifteen. Per game.

He was so dominant in that 1982-83 season that he won the MVP award again, this time as a 76er. Then the playoffs started and Moses made one of the most famous predictions in basketball history. More on that in Chapter 3. Just know this: Moses Malone arrived in Philadelphia and immediately made the 76ers the most feared team in the NBA. The whole league felt the shift the moment he signed.

9. Charles Barkley: Sir Charles (1984-1992)

Charles Barkley was listed at 6 feet 6 inches. This was, to put it charitably, optimistic. By some measurements he was closer to 6 feet 4. It did not matter even slightly. Barkley played power forward against centers who were four and five inches taller than him and regularly made them look like they had chosen the wrong career. He was built like a fire hydrant and moved like a point guard, and opposing big men spent a lot of time explaining to their coaches how they had gotten outrebounded by someone who could look them in the eye without standing on anything.

Barkley was drafted by Philadelphia with the fifth pick in the 1984 NBA Draft, the same draft that gave the world Michael Jordan, Hakeem Olajuwon, and John Stockton. He arrived as a teenager who was already one of the strongest players in the league and immediately became one of the most entertaining to watch. He scored, he rebounded, he talked, he argued with referees, and he made every single game more interesting than it would have been without him.

He spent eight seasons with the 76ers, made the All-Star team six times in Philadelphia, and never won a championship there, which remains one of the great what-ifs in franchise history. After he was traded to Phoenix in 1992 he won the NBA MVP award the very next season. The 76ers watched that from a distance and probably needed a moment.

10. Allen Iverson: The Answer (1996-2006, 2009-2010)

The 76ers drafted Allen Iverson with the first overall pick in 1996 and handed him a team that was not exactly loaded with talent. What followed over the next decade was one of the most remarkable individual performances in the history of professional basketball. Iverson was listed at 6 feet tall and approximately 165 pounds, which made him the smallest player at his position in the league by a significant margin. He responded to this by becoming one of the hardest players to stop that the NBA has ever seen.

He was not just quick. He was a different category of quick, the kind where defenders would set up in what seemed like a perfectly reasonable position and then Iverson was already past them before the information had reached their feet. He had a crossover dribble that was so fast and so sharp that it became genuinely controversial, with opposing coaches arguing it was an illegal carry on a semi-regular basis. The referees mostly disagreed. The ankle injuries of every defender who tried to stay in front of him agreed completely.

In 2001 Iverson won the NBA Most Valuable Player award, becoming one of the smallest players ever to claim that honor. He led the league in scoring four times. He carried the 76ers to the NBA Finals almost entirely on his own will, and in Game 1 he scored 48 points, hit a massive shot to force overtime, and then stepped over a defender named Tyronn Lue after knocking him down. That step-over became one of the defining images of his career and one of the most replayed moments in Finals history. Philadelphia has never had a player quite like him. Nobody has.

Chapter 3: The Moments That Defined the Sixers

11. Ending the Dynasty: The 1967 Playoffs

The Boston Celtics had won eight NBA championships in a row. Eight. That is not a dynasty. That is a hostage situation. Every other team in the league was basically showing up to compete for the right to lose to Boston in a slightly more dignified way. Coaches were drawing up game plans against the Celtics the way people write strongly-worded letters. Full of passion. Completely pointless.

Then the 1966-67 Philadelphia 76ers showed up and said enough. In the Eastern Division Finals they beat the Celtics five games to one. Not five games to four. Not a dramatic seven-game war. Five to one. The greatest dynasty in NBA history got handled like a homework assignment. Wilt Chamberlain was immovable. Hal Greer was automatic. Billy Cunningham played like he had a personal grudge against everyone wearing green.

Philadelphia went on to win the championship, beat the San Francisco Warriors in the Finals, and send a message to the entire league. The Celtics streak was dead. The throne had a new owner. And for one perfect season, the city of Philadelphia was the loudest place in basketball. Worth the wait. Absolutely worth the wait.

12. Fo, Fo, Fo: Moses and the 1983 Championship

Before the 1983 playoffs even tipped off, Moses Malone walked up to a microphone and made a prediction so bold it bordered on rude. He said the 76ers would sweep through every single playoff series, losing zero games along the way. Four games. Four games. Four games. In his Philadelphia accent it came out sounding like "fo, fo, fo," and those three syllables immediately became the most famous trash talk in 76ers history.

Here is the thing about making a massive public prediction before the playoffs. If you are wrong, people replay the clip forever and your face is attached to it every single time. They swept the Knicks. Swept the Bucks. Beat the Celtics four games to one. Swept the Lakers in the Finals. Three perfect sweeps and one series where Boston managed to steal a single game before Philadelphia closed them out anyway. Final record: 12 wins, one loss. Close enough to call it a prophecy.

The 1983 championship is still the last time Philadelphia has won it all. Moses called his shot, made his shot, and then left the city with a memory so good that fans are still talking about three syllables he said before a game forty years ago. Fo. Fo. Fo. Three words. One title. Legendary.

13. The Baseline Move: Dr. J in the 1980 Finals

The 76ers lost the 1980 NBA Finals to the Los Angeles Lakers. That is technically the result and we should probably mention it. But nobody remembers that part first, because in Game 4 Julius Erving did something so impossible that the people in the building spent a full second after it happened just trying to figure out what they had witnessed.

He caught the ball on the right baseline, drove hard toward the basket, and got cut off by a defender. Normal player stops, draws the foul, takes free throws, everyone goes home. Erving kept going. He took his entire body behind the backboard, lost sight of the rim completely, switched the ball to his left hand underneath the glass, floated back around the other side, and laid it in off the backboard as softly as if he had planned it from the beginning. The whole move took about two seconds. Physics filed a formal complaint.

Pretend you are sitting courtside. You watch Erving disappear behind the backboard and you think the play is dead. Then the ball goes in and half the arena starts laughing because they genuinely cannot believe what just happened. Magic Johnson said he could not believe it. Kareem Abdul-Jabbar just shook his head. The 76ers lost the series. Julius Erving won the highlight reel. And forty-five years later people are still watching that clip and losing their minds.

14. The Step-Over: Iverson in the 2001 Finals

The 2001 NBA Finals was supposed to be relaxing viewing for Lakers fans. Shaquille O'Neal. Kobe Bryant. Back-to-back champions. The 76ers were not supposed to win a single game, and several very confident television analysts said so out loud on national television, which Allen Iverson almost certainly heard.

Game 1. Iverson scores 48 points. He hits a shot with 1.4 seconds left in regulation to force overtime. The 76ers win. The entire basketball world stops and blinks. But the moment that made the highlight reel immortal happened when Iverson knocked Lakers guard Tyronn

Lue clean to the floor, and instead of waiting politely for him to get up, stepped directly over him and pointed downcourt to push the pace. Lue looked up from the hardwood. Iverson kept moving. The photograph of that moment ended up everywhere.

The 76ers lost the series four games to one. The Lakers were too deep, too rested, and too loaded. But nobody who watched Game 1 forgot it. A 165-pound point guard walked into the Staples Center, scored 48 points against the defending champions, and then literally stepped over one of their players like he was a speed bump. That is not a basketball play. That is a personality statement.

15. The Smallest MVP: Iverson Takes the Award (2001)

The NBA MVP award has historically gone to players who could be described using words like enormous, towering, and genuinely frightening. Kareem Abdul-Jabbar won it six times. Wilt Chamberlain won it four times. These were men who walked into a room and immediately made the ceiling feel lower. The trophy had a very clear type.

Allen Iverson won it at 6 feet tall and approximately 165 pounds. He showed up to the MVP conversation looking like someone who had wandered in through the wrong door and then refused to leave until they gave him the award. He led the entire NBA in scoring that season, averaging 31.1 points per game. He led the league in steals. He dragged a 76ers roster with almost no other reliable offensive weapons to the NBA Finals on sheer stubborn will and a crossover dribble that should have been declared a public safety hazard.

The voters looked at what he had done, looked at what everyone else had done, and handed him the trophy. The smallest guy in the room. The least likely candidate on paper. The one player every defender in the league had spent the season trying and failing to slow down. Iverson did not just win the MVP. He won it in a way that made the award feel personal, like the whole league had finally admitted what Philadelphia fans already knew. There was nobody else like him. There still isn't.

16. Franklin: The Blue Dog Who Was Designed by Kids

Every NBA team has a mascot. Some are intimidating. Some are majestic. The Philadelphia 76ers have a giant blue fluffy dog named Franklin, who was essentially designed by a committee of one thousand children between the ages of six and ten. The team handed the creative brief to the kids, asked them every possible question about fur color and size and whether he should dunk, and then built exactly what they described. The result is a large blue dog who does trampoline dunks at halftime and describes himself on social media as a fashionista and a movement savant.

The name is the best part. Franklin is named after Benjamin Franklin, Philadelphia's most famous founding father, which means the 76ers have now tied their entire identity to American history twice. Once with the team name. Once with the mascot. Other franchises name things after colors or animals. Philadelphia names things after the birth of a nation and the man who flew a kite in a lightning storm. It is a whole thing.

Franklin replaced Hip Hop, a rabbit who had been the mascot since 1998 and was retired in 2011 when new ownership decided it was time for a change. The kids wanted blue and fluffy and good at dunking. Franklin showed up and delivered all three. Philadelphia accepted him immediately, which for a city that once booed Santa Claus is basically a five-star review.

17. Trust the Process: The Rebuild That Broke the Internet

In 2013 the 76ers did something that no professional sports team had ever done quite so openly or so dramatically. They decided to be bad on purpose. Not accidentally bad. Not trying-their-best-but-coming-up-short bad. Deliberately, strategically, philosophically bad. The general manager at the time, Sam Hinkie, had a plan: lose enough games to collect high draft picks, use those picks to build something great, and accept years of pain in exchange for future glory. Philadelphia fans were asked to be patient. Philadelphia fans are not famous for patience.

The losses piled up. The 76ers set records for futility that nobody particularly wanted. There were seasons where winning felt like a surprise. The process was ugly. It was controversial. NBA executives debated it publicly. Fans either loved it or absolutely could not stand it.

Then Joel Embiid arrived. Then Ben Simmons arrived. Then the wins started coming and the playoff appearances returned and suddenly the plan had a name everybody knew. Embiid had called himself "The Process" on social media as a rookie, turning the whole painful rebuild into a rallying cry. Trust the Process became the motto. The t-shirts sold out. The rebuild that divided the NBA ended up producing a player who won the MVP award. Sometimes being bad on purpose turns out to be a very good idea.

18. The Boo Birds: Philadelphia's Toughest Crowd

Philadelphia fans are not mean. They are just extremely honest, and they will share that honesty with you immediately, loudly, and from a seat that is surprisingly close to the court. Other cities have passionate fanbases. Philadelphia has a fanbase that once booed Santa Claus. Not a bad Santa. Not a late Santa. A perfectly normal Santa Claus who showed up at an Eagles game in 1968 and got absolutely pelted with snowballs by people who apparently had strong feelings about the holiday season. Santa Claus. They booed Santa Claus.

Playing for Philadelphia means understanding the deal from day one. When things are going well the Wells Fargo Center is one of the loudest and most electric buildings in the NBA. When things are going badly the crowd will let you know with a speed and specificity that no coach's halftime speech could ever match. Players have been booed during introductions. Players have been booed during warmups. There is a version of Philadelphia fandom where getting booed means they still care, and that is somehow both a threat and a compliment at the same time.

The remarkable thing is that it works. Players who survive Philadelphia and earn that crowd's respect earn something that no other fanbase in America can give them. When Philly loves you they love you completely and permanently. Allen Iverson left, came back, and got a standing ovation every single time he touched the ball. That is the other side of the boo birds. Earn it in Philadelphia and you have earned it forever.

19. Wells Fargo Center: Loud, Proud, and Absolutely Not Quiet

The Wells Fargo Center opened in 1996 and has been one of the louder buildings in the NBA ever since, for reasons that have everything to do with the city it sits in. Philadelphia fans do not attend games as passive observers. They attend games as participants, judges, and occasionally as the loudest sound in the entire building. When things are going well the place is electric. When things are going badly the crowd lets the players know immediately, specifically, and at significant volume.

The arena holds around 20,000 fans for basketball and sits in South Philadelphia alongside Lincoln Financial Field and Citizens Bank Park, meaning there is a square mile of that city that on any given weekend contains more passionate sports fans per square foot than almost anywhere else on earth. The parking lots alone have generated more sports arguments than most cities produce in an entire season. Philly fans travel in groups and they have opinions.

The building has hosted two NBA Finals, countless playoff runs, and one very famous night in 2001 when Allen Iverson carried the city on his back so many times that the crowd basically refused to go home afterward. Great arenas have personalities. The Wells Fargo Center's personality is that it will absolutely cheer you and absolutely boo you and it will mean both completely sincerely. Welcome to Philadelphia. They hope you can handle it.

20. The Wall of Retired Numbers

When a franchise retires a player's number it means nobody on that team will ever wear it again. It goes up in the rafters, it stays there forever, and every time a rookie looks up during warmups they get a reminder of exactly whose house they are playing in. The 76ers have sent a lot of numbers to the rafters, and the list reads like a hall of fame greatest hits album.

Number 6 belongs to Julius Erving. Number 13 belongs to Wilt Chamberlain. Number 15 belongs to Hal Greer, who was so consistently excellent for so long that people sometimes forget to mention him when listing the franchise's greatest players, which is genuinely unfair to Hal Greer. Number 24 belongs to Bobby Jones. Number 32 belongs to Billy Cunningham. Number 34 belongs to Charles Barkley, who was traded away and still got his number retired, which tells you everything you need to know about how Philadelphia felt about Sir Charles. And number 3 belongs to Allen Iverson, who never won a championship in a 76ers uniform and still got one of the loudest retirement ceremonies the building has ever seen.

Each of those numbers represents a player who did something so memorable for this franchise that Philadelphia decided to close the door on that jersey permanently. Most relationships do not last that long. The 76ers look up at that wall every single night and play in front of it, which is either deeply inspiring or mildly terrifying. Probably both. Definitely both.

Chapter 5: The Sixers Today and Tomorrow

21. Joel Embiid: From Cameroon to the Center of the NBA

Joel Embiid grew up in Yaoundé, Cameroon, where basketball was not exactly the national obsession. He did not pick up a basketball until he was sixteen years old. Sixteen. Most NBA players have been dribbling since they could walk. Embiid spent his early teenage years playing volleyball and soccer, which means there is a parallel universe somewhere where a 7-foot center is currently dominating the volleyball world and nobody there knows what they have.

A scout saw him play in 2011 and immediately started making phone calls. Within a year Embiid had moved to the United States, started training seriously, and begun the process of becoming one of the most skilled big men the NBA has ever seen. He could shoot from the perimeter. He could post up. He could pass. He had footwork that made opposing centers look like they were wearing shoes on the wrong feet. All of this after less than five years of playing the sport.

The 76ers drafted him third overall in 2014 and then waited. Embiid missed his first two seasons with foot injuries that would have derailed most careers before they started. He sat. He rehabbed. He posted extremely entertaining things on social media. And then he came back, and Philadelphia discovered that the wait had been completely worth it. A kid from Cameroon who had never touched a basketball at fourteen years old was about to become the face of one of the most historic franchises in the sport.

22. The Process Pays Off: Embiid's MVP (2022-23)

Remember all those losses? All those terrible seasons? All those games where the 76ers finished with a score that looked more like a weather temperature than a basketball result? All of that, every single painful loss, was supposedly part of the plan. Trust the Process. And then in the 2022-23 season Joel Embiid went out and won the NBA Most Valuable Player award, which was either proof that the plan worked or the most expensive way in sports history to develop one really good player. Possibly both.

Embiid averaged 33.1 points, 10.2 rebounds, and 4.2 assists per game that season, numbers so good they looked like a typo. He was dominant in a way that made people run out of new words to describe him. He scored from everywhere. He defended. He set screens that removed defenders from the game both legally and philosophically. He had developed a post game so complete that coaches trying to scheme against him were basically choosing which problem they wanted to have rather than solving any of them.

The MVP trophy was the official receipt for years of rebuilding, losing, and asking fans to be patient in a city that treats patience like a foreign language. Sam Hinkie had drafted the plan in 2013. Embiid delivered the trophy ten years later. The Process worked. It just took long enough that several people involved at the beginning were no longer around to celebrate, which is either poetic or deeply ironic depending on how you feel about front office drama.

23. Philly vs. Boston: The Rivalry That Refuses to Die

The Philadelphia 76ers and the Boston Celtics have been making each other miserable since the 1960s and show absolutely no signs of stopping. This is not one of those polite rivalries where both teams respect each other deeply and compete with dignity. This is a rivalry where fans on both sides have spent sixty years accumulating very specific grievances that they can recite from memory at any hour of the day or night.

It started when the 76ers ended Boston's eight-championship dynasty in 1967 and the Celtics decided that was unacceptable. It continued through the 1980s when both teams were loaded and beating each other up in the playoffs on a near-annual basis. It reignited in the modern era when the 76ers rebuilt through the Process and started competing again, which meant more playoff series, more drama, and more opportunities for fans of both cities to yell at each other on the internet with tremendous dedication.

Philadelphia has beaten Boston in moments that felt historic. Boston has beaten Philadelphia in moments that felt catastrophic. The series always seem to go deep, always seem to produce at least one sequence that gets replayed for years, and always seem to end with someone somewhere absolutely furious about it. Some rivalries are about geography. Some are about history. The Sixers and Celtics rivalry is both, plus a grudge that has now been passed down through multiple generations of fans who inherited it like a family heirloom nobody asked for but everyone carries anyway.

24. Three Championships, Three Completely Different Teams

The Philadelphia 76ers have won three NBA championships. What makes that remarkable is not the number, although three is perfectly respectable. What makes it remarkable is that those three titles were won by three teams that had almost nothing in common except the city name on the front of the jersey.

The 1955 championship was won by the Syracuse Nationals, a scrappy mid-market team led by Dolph Schayes that most people outside of upstate New York had to look up on a map to find. The 1967 championship was won by a historically dominant 68-win team built around the most physically imposing player the sport had ever seen. The 1983 championship was won by a team whose entire identity changed the moment Moses Malone walked through the door and started grabbing every rebound that came within fifteen feet of him.

Three eras. Three completely different rosters. Three completely different styles of basketball separated by decades of the sport evolving in different directions. The only constants were the uniform, the city, and the standard those teams set every time they went out and won it all. Banner number four has been the goal for over forty years now. The fans are still waiting. They are not quiet about it.

25. The Next Chapter: Philadelphia Is Not Done

Here is the thing about Philadelphia 76ers fans. They are not casual. They are not the kind of people who show up when things are going well and disappear when they are not. They show up regardless, loud regardless, and convinced regardless that this is the year things turn around. This is a city that once booed Santa Claus at an Eagles game, which tells you everything you need to know about the standards they hold everyone to, including Saint Nicholas.

The 76ers have all the ingredients for another run. Joel Embiid is one of the most skilled centers the league has ever produced. The roster around him has been rebuilt, retooled, and reconsidered multiple times in pursuit of finding the right combination. Every offseason brings new moves, new names, and new reasons for Philadelphia fans to either feel electric about the future or spend three months arguing about it on sports radio, sometimes both within the same week.

The history is there. The banners are up. The retired numbers on the wall represent some of the greatest players the sport has ever produced. The city is ready, has always been ready, and will remain ready until the day someone in a 76ers uniform lifts that trophy again. And when that day comes, the Wells Fargo Center is going to be so loud they will hear it in Syracuse. Which feels exactly right.

Bonus Trivia Quiz!

You think you are a true 76ers fan? Try this bonus quiz!

1. The team that became the Philadelphia 76ers originally played in which city?

A) Buffalo

B) Syracuse

C) Rochester

D) Hartford

2. What year did the Syracuse Nationals win the NBA Championship?

A) 1951

B) 1953

C) 1955

D) 1957

3. How did the 76ers get their name?

A) The owner's lucky number was 76

B) The team was founded in 1876

C) A fan contest chose the name as a reference to 1776 and the Declaration of Independence

D) There were 76 original season ticket holders

4. What was the 76ers' regular season record during their legendary 1966-67 championship season?

A) 62-18

B) 65-15

C) 68-13

D) 70-12

5. Wilt Chamberlain scored 100 points in a single game in 1962. Who holds the second highest single-game scoring record in NBA history as of 2026?

A) Kobe Bryant

B) Elgin Baylor

C) Bam Adebayo

D) David Thompson

6. Julius Erving came to the 76ers from which team when the ABA merged with the NBA?

A) Denver Nuggets

B) Indiana Pacers

C) Kentucky Colonels

D) New York Nets

7. What was Moses Malone's famous playoff prediction before the 1983 postseason?

A) We will win every game by double digits
B) Fo, fo, fo
C) Nobody can stop us, nobody
D) Four straight sweeps, guaranteed

8. How many games did the 76ers lose in the entire 1983 playoffs?

A) Zero
B) One
C) Two
D) Three

9. In the 1980 NBA Finals, Julius Erving made his famous baseline move against which team?

A) Boston Celtics
B) Seattle SuperSonics
C) Los Angeles Lakers
D) Houston Rockets

10. How many points did Allen Iverson score in Game 1 of the 2001 NBA Finals?

A) 38

B) 42

C) 45

D) 48

11. Which Lakers player did Allen Iverson step over during the 2001 NBA Finals?

A) Kobe Bryant

B) Rick Fox

C) Tyronn Lue

D) Derek Fisher

12. What nickname did Joel Embiid give himself on social media that became the entire franchise's rallying cry?

A) The Big Man

B) The Future

C) The Process

D) The Answer

13. Which of these numbers has NOT been retired by the 76ers?

A) Number 6 (Julius Erving)
B) Number 33 (Kareem Abdul-Jabbar)
C) Number 34 (Charles Barkley)
D) Number 3 (Allen Iverson)

14. Where did Joel Embiid grow up before moving to the United States?

A) Nigeria
B) France
C) Senegal
D) Cameroon

15. Which season did Joel Embiid win the NBA Most Valuable Player award?

A) 2019-20
B) 2020-21
C) 2022-23
D) 2021-22

Super Fan Secret Challenge

Only a true 76ers fan will know this.

(No Answer Provided)

Only one person in Philadelphia 76ers history has won an NBA championship with the franchise as both a player and a head coach. Who is he, and in which two years did he win?

A) Alex Hannum, 1955 and 1967
B) Billy Cunningham, 1967 and 1983
C) Jack Ramsay, 1967 and 1977
D) Larry Brown, 1983 and 2001

Answer Key

1. B) Syracuse

2. C) 1955

3. C) A fan contest chose the name as a reference to 1776 and the Declaration of Independence

4. C) 68-13

5. C) Bam Adebayo

6. D) New York Nets

7. B) Fo, fo, fo

8. B) One

9. C) Los Angeles Lakers

10. D) 48

11. C) Tyronn Lue

12. C) The Process

13. B) Number 33 (Kareem Abdul-Jabbar)

14. D) Cameroon

15. C) 2022-23

NBA PLAYOFF BRACKET

First Round | Semifinals | Conf. Finals | Finals | Conf. Finals | Semifinals | First Round

* Fill in your picks and try not to argue with your friends about it!

Part of the Fun Fan Facts: The Unofficial Sports Guide Series

Be the Boss of the Playoffs

You've broken down the matchups. You know which superstar takes over in the fourth quarter. You've seen the bench units that quietly decide series. You've watched the adjustments coaches make when their backs are against the wall.

Now it's time to stop watching and start deciding.

On this page, you are not just a fan. You are the Head Coach drawing up the last play with three seconds left on the clock. You are the GM who built this roster. You are the analyst who saw it all coming.

This is not just filling out a bracket.

This is building your championship run.

Sixteen teams enter the NBA Playoffs. The path is brutal. Best of seven. No shortcuts. No hiding. Every round gets louder, harder, and more personal.

This bracket is your Playoff Control Room.

The Game Plan

1. Survive Round One: Start with the opening round. Which matchup is going seven games? Who has the closer? Who folds under pressure? Make the calls.

2. Feel the Momentum: As you move into the Conference Semifinals and Conference Finals, things change. Role players become heroes. Stars feel the weight. Trust your reads.

3. Own the Finals: Trace your picks all the way to the NBA Finals. When the confetti falls and the trophy is raised, you'll find out who earned it.

House Rules: Circle your boldest upset. That is your official "I knew it" moment.

Choose Your Weapon: Pencil if you want flexibility. Pen if you trust your instincts. Sharpie if you believe in chaos.

Because once the playoffs tip off, there is no rewinding Game 7.

Make your picks. Trust your basketball brain. And let the playoff drama begin.

Fun Facts Wrap-Up

You made it through! You're officially a true superfan! Now it's time to put your knowledge to the test. Share these facts with friends and see who really knows their team best.

Love the series?

Your reviews help other fans discover Fun Fan Facts. If you enjoyed this book, we'd really appreciate you sharing your thoughts and leaving a review.

Want more Fun Fan Facts?

Scan the QR code below to visit our site and explore bonus trivia, challenges, and special extras - including new teams, future series, and collectible fun as they're released.

Collect All the Fun Fan Facts Series!

Check off every book you read. See the full set on Amazon. Search "Fun Fan Facts Jake Liam."

World Cup 2026 Edition

☐ Algeria	☐ Scotland	☐ Morocco
☐ France	☐ Brazil	☐ Switzerland
☐ Paraguay	☐ Ivory Coast	☐ Curaçao
☐ Argentina	☐ Senegal	☐ Netherlands
☐ Germany	☐ Canada	☐ Tunisia
☐ Portugal	☐ Japan	☐ Ecuador
☐ Australia	☐ South Africa	☐ New Zealand
☐ Ghana	☐ Cape Verde	☐ United States
☐ Qatar	☐ Jordan	☐ Egypt
☐ Austria	☐ South Korea	☐ Norway
☐ Haiti	☐ Colombia	☐ Uruguay
☐ Saudi Arabia	☐ Mexico	☐ England
☐ Belgium	☐ Spain	☐ Panama
☐ Iran	☐ Croatia	☐ Uzbekistan

World Cup 2026 Group Edition

☐ Group A	☐ Group F	☐ Group K
☐ Group E	☐ Group J	☐ Group D
☐ Group I	☐ Group C	☐ Group H
☐ Group B	☐ Group G	☐ Group L

English Football Edition

☐ Arsenal F.C.

☐ Aston Villa F.C.

☐ Chelsea F.C.

☐ Everton F.C.

☐ Fulham F.C.

☐ Liverpool F.C.

☐ Manchester City

☐ Manchester United

☐ Newcastle United F.C.

☐ Tottenham Hotspur

☐ West Ham United

☐ Wrexham A.F.C.

NBA Edition

☐ Atlanta Hawks

☐ Boston Celtics

☐ Brooklyn Nets

☐ Charlotte Hornets

☐ Chicago Bulls

☐ Cleveland Cavaliers

☐ Dallas Mavericks

☐ Denver Nuggets

☐ Detroit Pistons

☐ Golden State Warriors

☐ Houston Rockets

☐ Indiana Pacers

☐ LA Clippers

☐ Los Angeles Lakers

☐ Memphis Grizzlies

☐ Miami Heat

☐ Milwaukee Bucks

☐ Minnesota Timberwolves

☐ New Orleans Pelicans

☐ New York Knicks

☐ Oklahoma City Thunder

☐ Orlando Magic

☐ Philadelphia 76ers

☐ Phoenix Suns

☐ Portland Trail Blazers

☐ Sacramento Kings

☐ San Antonio Spurs

☐ Toronto Raptors

☐ Utah Jazz

☐ Washington Wizards

About the Author

Jake is a 13-year-old sports fan who loves football, American football, and basketball. He plays soccer as a goalie and dreams of one day playing for West Ham United and helping teach kids to love the game. His passion for sports runs in the family - his dad was a professional baseball player, and his stepdad sparked his love for West Ham. Through the Fun Fan Facts series, he shares the fun and excitement of sports with fans everywhere.